CRYSTAL STAR ANGEL

by

Anita Joyce Skocz

Illustrated by Cynthia Lee Christy

PAULIST PRESS
New York/Mahwah, NJ

Library of Congress Cataloging-in-Publication Data

Skocz, Anita Joyce, 1952-
    Crystal star angel / by Anita Joyce Skocz; illustrated by Cynthia Lee Christy.
        p.   cm.
    Summary: Larry brings all of his quarreling neighbors together at Christmas and receives the angelic Crystal Star for his peace-making.
    ISBN 0-8091-6617-8 (pbk.)
    [1. Christmas—Fiction. 2. Angels—Fiction. 3. Anger—Fiction.] I. Christy, Cynthia Lee, ill.
II. Title.
PZ7.S62834Cr   1994
[E]—dc20   94-13811
                                                                                                       CIP
                                                                                                        AC

Published by Paulist Press
997 Macarthur Boulevard
Mahwah, New Jersey 07430

Printed and bound in the
United States of America

This book is dedicated to my nephew, Larry Smith.
His loving nature has inspired this story,
and has opened the hearts of many.

It was a beautiful brisk sunny Florida day, and with Christmas only two days away, Larry glowed with the excitement of the season. As he played in his backyard, Larry could smell all the spicy aromas coming from his mother's busy kitchen.

Larry stopped to listen. He thought he heard someone crying near the big oak tree. Not knowing what he would find, Larry walked very slowly toward the tree. He looked curiously around the trunk and his eyes opened wide in total surprise.

There, sitting on a rock, was a tiny and beautiful girl.

"Who are you?" asked Larry with a puzzled look on his face.

The girl wiped her eyes; she tried to speak, but tears kept rolling down her pink cheeks.

Finally, she looked at Larry, and quietly said, "I'm a Crystal Star Angel."

Larry had heard of angels in stories, but had never seen one. He wasn't sure what he should do.

"Would you like to come and meet my mother?" Larry asked.

The angel smiled, and shook her head no. Then she explained. "Grown-ups can't see Crystal Star Angels. Only children can see me, Larry."

Larry shook his head in surprise. "How did you know my name?"

The angel laughed. "Oh, angels know all children's names. That's part of our job."

Larry was filled with questions, but first he asked, "Why were you crying?"

The angel wondered if she should tell Larry, but seeing he was truly concerned, she began her story.

"Well, Larry, I have a big problem; I can't get back to heaven. Every year one hundred angels are selected to come to earth, and pass out Crystal Stars. We are to find a child and follow him or her for twenty-four hours. If the child behaves in a loving way for the entire time, we present the child with an award, the Crystal Star. It is a magical star, which glows brilliantly when it is placed on a Christmas tree. And each person who is touched by the light is filled with peace and love for all. The other angels are already back in heaven preparing for the Christmas celebration, but I haven't found a child who's been loving and caring."

The angel's story saddened Larry; he didn't want her to miss the big celebration. He closed his eyes and tried to think of a way to help her. To his surprise, when he opened them the angel had disappeared!

Larry searched the whole yard, but he couldn't find the angel anywhere. Just then, his mother called him into the house. She could tell that Larry was unhappy, so she asked, "Why the sad face, Peanut?"

Larry knew that nobody would believe his story, so he just smiled and said nothing about the angel. Larry's Mom gave him some cookbooks to take to his Grandma's house and he raced out the door, with the thought of the angel fresh on his mind.

Grandma lived close by, and Larry knew all the neighbors along the way. Everyone knew Larry too, and his warm smile always brightened their darkest day.

While Larry walked today, he had a strange feeling. He felt as though someone was following him, but nobody was there.

The first house that Larry passed was Mr. Spanelli's. He had a green thumb, and the prettiest flowers in the whole neighborhood to prove it. As Larry walked by, Mr. Spanelli called out.

"Hello there, Larry, it's a beautiful day!"

Larry smiled, and walked over to see him. "I love your flowers, Mr. Spanelli. They look like a hundred smiling faces."

Mr. Spanelli was pleased by Larry's remark, but his smile faded and an angry look took its place.

"They are beautiful Larry, and I work so very hard to keep them smiling. But . . . but . . . that cat, that cat of Ms. Greenly's keeps digging in my flower bed. And . . . well . . . well, she never does anything about it!"

Larry knew that Mr. Spanelli and Ms. Greenly weren't speaking, but now he knew why.

"Did you see the cat digging, Mr. Spanelli?"

"No . . . no, I haven't, but I know it's her sneaky little cat."

Mr. Spanelli kept mumbling about the cat. Larry, a bit frightened, decided to say good-bye. He wished Mr. Spanelli and Ms. Greenly would take time and talk about their problem, but it didn't look hopeful.

While Larry continued, Gus, the mailman, approached him.

"Hi Gus!" said Larry with a warm and glowing smile.

Gus usually teased Larry with a trick, or a riddle, but today was different. Gus wasn't very jolly.

"Hi, Larry, would you do me a favor . . . and . . . well . . . take your Grandma's mail for me?"

"Sure, Gus, but why?" Larry asked, while reaching for the mail.

Gus shook his head back and forth very slowly. "You won't believe it, but your Grandma and I are not speaking."

"Why?" asked Larry, almost afraid of the answer.

"Well . . . I . . . ah . . . guess I went too far with my joking. While your Grandma sang Christmas carols with all her heart, I hid behind the fence and howled like a dog."

Larry crossed his eyes, and threw up his hands. "Oh, Gus, Grandma has such a beautiful voice, that must have hurt her."

Gus lowered his eyes and said, "I figured that out . . . when . . . when she stopped singing. We haven't talked in days, and to be quite honest . . . I . . . I miss her tall tales."

With a sad look on his face Larry walked away. Christmas was two days away, and he wondered if there was anything he could do to settle all the differences.

With this on his mind, Larry's pace was slower as he continued toward Grandma's house. After a few steps he stopped and turned; he still felt as though someone was following him, but all he saw was Gus off in the distance.

Shrugging his shoulders he continued; he tried to enjoy the Christmas decorations along the way, but the spirit of the holiday was missing. The neighbors seemed as though they had lost sight of the love, peace and joy of the season.

When Larry reached his Grandma's house, his Grandpa was hanging a wreath on the front door.

"Hi, Grandpa, that's a lovely decoration!"

Larry's Grandpa did not say a word.

"What's the matter?" Larry asked with concern.

"Oh, nothing . . . well, yes . . . it's . . . it's Grandma," Grandpa said nervously, while making sure Grandma wasn't listening.

"Grandma wanted the wreath in the window; I wanted the wreath on the door. Before I could give my reasons . . . she . . . she slammed the door, and now she won't speak to me."

Larry started to understand why the angel was having trouble. Everyone he saw today seemed to be mad about silly little things. He began to wonder if all grown-ups were this unhappy around Christmas.

When Larry entered the house, he found his Grandma working quietly in the kitchen. Seeing Larry she smiled and spoke.

"Well, I'm sure glad to see someone with a smiling face today!"

Grandma took the books and mail from Larry, and before he could say a word, she placed a plate of oatmeal cookies and a tall glass of milk in front of him.

"You always know when I'm ready for a treat!" Larry said, picking up his first cookie.

Grandma laughed. "That's not hard to do; you're always hungry!"

As Larry ate the cookies, he could see the sadness in his Grandma's eyes. Her joyful spirit wasn't there, and that seemed strange so close to Christmas.

"Thanks, Grandma!" Larry shouted, while running out the door.

Thinking of the angel, and hoping she had solved her problem, Larry walked home slowly.

As he turned the corner, he noticed Mrs. Foster's newspaper lying in her driveway. This seemed odd, because Mrs. Foster always got up with the sun, and her cheery piano tunes usually filled the air. Putting the newspaper in his hand, Larry stepped toward the door.

"Mrs. Foster . . . it's Larry. Are . . . are you home?

Mrs. Foster came to the door wiping her eyes. Handing her the paper, Larry asked, "What's the matter . . . why are you crying?"

Mrs. Foster said sadly, "Oh, it's my daughter, Suzy; she can't make it home for Christmas, and . . . she's all the family I have."

Mrs. Foster wiped again, then went on, saying, "She usually puts up my tree, and bakes all kinds of treats. Well . . . well, she's the one that puts life into this old house. I guess it will just be Lucky and me."

Lucky was good company but Larry knew a dog was not the same as Mrs. Foster's daughter.

"Please drop by Christmas day. My Mom has made plenty of treats, and I'm sure she would love having you visit."

Mrs. Foster thanked Larry for the invitation. He continued home feeling quite blue.

He thought to himself. "There must be something I can do." Then . . . like a flash . . . an idea came to mind.

Without saying a word Larry rushed into his house, and right into his room. He put his piggy bank in his wagon, and ran out the door.

"I'm going to the corner to wait for the school bus to drop off Karen," Larry yelled.

"OK, Larry, be careful!" Larry's Mom replied.

When Larry reached the corner, he waited patiently for Karen, his babysitter. He wasn't allowed to leave his neighborhood without a grown-up, so he hoped Karen would help him with his idea.

In minutes the big yellow school bus pulled up with a squeak of its brakes. All the high school students poured out of the bus laughing and talking. Karen spotted Larry.

"What are you doing here, Larry?"

Larry grabbed her hand and pulled her out of the crowd.

"Oh, Karen . . . I . . . I need you to help me," Larry said in a hurry. "I . . . I've got to get to Main Street . . . uh . . . to buy a tree . . . please, please go with me."

Karen was confused. "Larry, you have a tree, and it's been up for weeks."

Larry rattled on.

"The tree isn't for my family, it's . . . it's for Mrs. Foster."

Karen agreed to walk with Larry. He told her all about his day with the neighbors, and he shared his idea with her, too.

When they reached the tree lot, Larry took his piggy bank, and marched straight up to Mr. Lewis, the sales clerk.

"I would like to buy a tree, but I'm not sure how much I have here."

Karen explained the whole story to Mr. Lewis. After hearing it, he scratched his head, then said, "Well, Larry, I think I have the perfect tree for you."

Larry's excitement grew, and Karen beamed with excitement, too. In a few moments the salesman returned with a tree. It was beautiful.

"How much do I owe you, sir?" Larry asked, while clutching his bank.

"Well, it's two days until Christmas . . . and, uh . . . I still have plenty of trees. I think I can let it go for twenty-five cents."

Larry and Karen thanked Mr. Lewis for helping them, and off they went. Pulling the tree behind them, they sang their favorite Christmas songs.

Larry raced to the phone when he got home. He had to call Mr. Spanelli, Gus, Ms. Greenly, his Grandma and his Grandpa. His idea was to invite them over to Mrs. Foster's to help decorate her tree. Of course, they were all delighted to come. However, Larry didn't tell Mr. Spanelli that Ms. Greenly would be there. He also neglected to tell Gus and Grandpa that his Grandma would be there. His plan was to get them all together, and hope that the spirit of Christmas would settle their differences.

Last, Larry called Mrs. Foster. He wanted to let her know he'd be dropping by on Christmas eve afternoon.

While Larry slept, the Crystal Star Angel smiled over his bed. She knew that she had found a loving, caring child to give the star to.

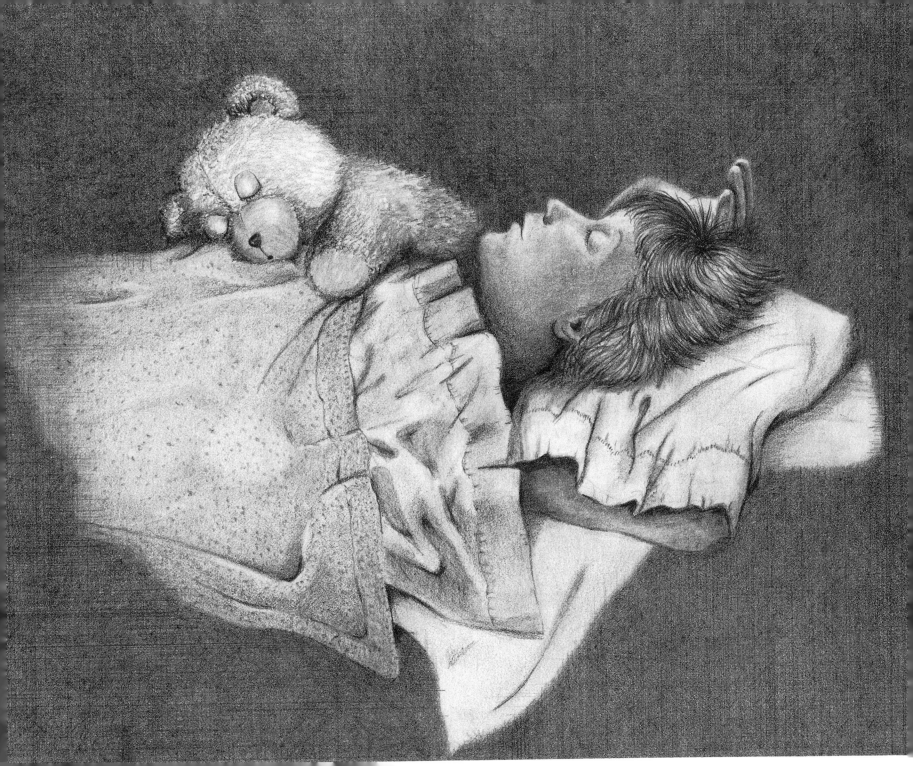

The next morning Larry jumped out of bed early. After breakfast he went out to check the tree and wait for Karen. She offered to help Larry secure the tree stand.

Larry kept looking over his shoulder. He felt sure someone was watching him, yet nobody was around.

Karen arrived with the old stand and they worked together to prepare the tree.

When they finished, Larry thanked Karen . . . and off he went.

With the tree in the wagon, and the Christmas spirit in his heart, Larry walked happily down the street.

As he knocked at Mrs. Foster's door, he could hear the dog racing toward the entrance with Mrs. Foster right behind.

"Well, good morning, Larry," Mrs. Foster said with a puzzled look in her eyes. She spotted the tree, and wondered what Larry had in mind.

"Good morning, Mrs. Foster . . . ahhh . . . Mr. Lewis was selling his trees for a quarter . . . and . . . well . . . I thought maybe you would enjoy having one."

Before Mrs. Foster could respond, Gus came whistling up the sidewalk.

"Well, I see we have a handsome looking tree to trim. Shall we carry it in and dress it for Christmas?"

When she realized what Larry planned to do, tears came to Mrs. Foster's eyes.

Gus lifted the tree effortlessly, and before Mrs. Foster could blink an eye, the tree stood regally next to her fireplace.

Mrs. Foster's face took on a childlike expression as she ran out of the room shouting, "I'll be right back with all my favorite ornaments."

Now there was another knock at the door. In came Grandpa with a big pine cone wreath in his hands.

"Good to see you, Gus," said Grandpa. "Are you going to help with the decorating too?"

Gus winked and replied, "I sure am!"

Before Gus could say another word, the door flew open and in marched Grandma with a basket filled with cookies. Grandma looked at Gus and Grandpa, and with a disturbed look in her eyes, she walked past both of them.

After placing her bundle down, Grandma grumbled at Grandpa. "Well . . . if I knew you were going to be here . . . well . . . well, I never would have come!"

Gus was feeling quite uncomfortable after teasing Grandma, and she could tell it from the embarrassed look on his face.

Right behind Grandma came Mr. Spanelli.

"Good afternoon, everyone. I didn't know that all you Santa's helpers would be here."

Grandma, Grandpa and Gus were quiet, and soon Mr. Spanelli's cheery expression changed too. There, coming in the door with her cat, was Ms. Greenly. Mr. Spanelli couldn't control himself.

"Who invited you . . . you and that nasty ol' cat?"

Ms. Greenly laughed. "Neighbor, you need your eyes tested. The raccoon that's been dancing in your flower bed doesn't even look like my precious kitty!"

Within moments everyone in the room began shouting. Grandpa started arguing with Grandma, and Gus joined in, too. Mr. Spanelli and Ms. Greenly had their fingers shaking in each other's faces . . . each trying to have the last word.

While everyone stood there arguing, Larry's mother arrived. It didn't take her long to realize that Larry had a part in this confusion. Before he could explain, Larry was being scolded by his mother.

Just then Mrs. Foster returned with the decorations.

"What happened to the Christmas spirit?" she exclaimed.

But the noise grew louder, and nobody could hear her. Even Lucky left the room, saddened by all the anger.

Mrs. Foster's eyes began to tear again. Seeing her sadness, Larry spoke out.

"I thought Christmas was a time of love. Why is everyone being so hateful?"

Realizing what Larry was trying to do, everyone became silent. At the same time a brilliant light flooded the room. The power of its glow was dazzling, and all eyes fluttered and closed. Slowly, the light dimmed, and everyone looked toward Larry. They understood then that love had sparked his idea. Peace and warmth were felt by everyone.

Grandma hugged Grandpa tightly, and with a twinkle in her eyes winked at Gus. Smiling, Mr. Spanelli walked over to Ms. Greenly, and they began talking and laughing with each other. At the same time Larry's Mom came up to him, and gave him a big kiss. She said proudly, "You gave us all the greatest gift, Peanut, the gift of love."

Larry's wish came true. Everyone was touched by the spirit of Christmas. The ladies made punch and put cookies out, and joined the men in decorating the tree.

While Larry watched his friends and family, his eyes caught sight of the top of the tree. Hanging there, sparkling in all directions, was the Crystal Star. "Of course!" he thought to himself. "It was the Crystal Star Angel."

Before he could blink an eye, Larry heard someone calling him. He looked to the right of the star, and there, surrounded in a rainbow of colors, hovered the Angel. Her eyes twinkled with a loving glow as she waved good-by and said,

"MERRY CHRISTMAS, LARRY!"

Larry smiled, and waved heartily, knowing that she could return now for the big celebration.

He thought the day was perfect, when the door flew open one more time. Standing with an armful of packages was Mrs. Foster's daughter, Suzy.

"MERRY CHRISTMAS, MOM," Suzy shouted.

Mrs. Foster grabbed her daughter, and held her tightly. All the neighbors greeted Suzy warmly. She thanked everyone for making her mother's Christmas a joyous one.

Although Larry was only eight years old, he had taken his idea. . . and twenty-five cents . . . and brought the spirit of Christmas back into the hearts of his friends and family.